Professional Services 101

Surviving and Thriving During Your First Year

Christopher B. Horn

Some of what is contained herein I figured out myself. The majority of it I learned from others. For that, I would like to thank (chronologically):

My parents, Mike Bennett, Ed Hill, Steve Vezendy, Mike Villegas, Tom Wallace, Pam Troy-Kopack, Eric Trapp, Mike Suba (believe it or not, I actually learned things from you), Bob Mecca, Mike Carper, Mike Brown, Lynn Blecha, Rick Hazen, Bill Barrett, Tom Bussa, Larry Rodriguez, Tim Esaki, Jason Nagai, Andrew Ellis, Jela Foote, Steve Singer, Dan Sernett, Joanie Lebedeff, Frank Ellis, my dad (again), Linda (Peggy) Kirby, Ken Hammond, KJ Kuchta, Peter Brady, Scott Pelle, Yanna Ma, John Lanza, Andrew Bannon, Evan Tripp, Sergio de la Fe, Shalerie Brady, Patricia Mount, Savina Waldron, Lou Musto, Allan Cohen, Rob Kastenschmidt, A. Michael Smith, Kim Powell, Bharath Kumar VankipuramPartha and Jack McNamara. I probably forgot a few – Sorry!

The transformation of a large pile of notes and thoughts into a book was aided immensely by several people who read my early drafts and provided much needed comments and suggestions. In no particular order, I am grateful to Mike Suba, Lou Musto, Peter Brady, Terry Risley, Scott Pelle, Shalerie Brady, Bill Barrett, David Bright, Lynn Blecha, Carol Lapidus, Mary Beth Mulligan and Sandra Horn. Again, if I forget anyone, please forgive me.

Finally, I would like to thank Mary Beth Mulligan for writing the section on Dressing for work (Women). There is no way I was going to try to give women advice on how to dress.

Contents

Forward

This book is written for individuals who are about to enter, or have just entered a career in professional services. I have spent a significant portion of my professional life in this industry, mostly with public accounting firms, and can honestly say that I have loved almost every aspect of my job, almost every day.

The single responsibility I have enjoyed the most about my work experience is the recruitment and development of new staff associates. I have worked directly with hundreds of first-year staff people over the last 25 years, and have helped them deal with just about every aspect of their assimilation into their new position. This book is intended to provide you with the exact same advice I have given them. I have not tried to cover everything you will need to know – I have just focused on areas where I have consistently provided advice.

You have chosen to start your career in a fantastic place. Whether you stay with your current employer for two years or for the rest of your career, what you do in your first year will help you set the pace for your career path. Make the most of it!

Good luck,

Chris

How to read this book

This book is intended to be used as a reference, and it is organized to allow you to quickly locate sections or specific topics.

If this is the first time you have opened the book up, read it cover to cover to familiarize yourself with the material. Keep the book with you so that you can refer back to it when you need to. For instance, before you go shopping for work clothes, read the pertinent sections in **Chapter 2: Clothing**. The first few times you are going to run a meeting, flip to page 59 and review the section entitled "Running meetings" to help you prepare. You get the idea. The chapters are color coded to allow you to easily flip to a specific chapter, and for more detail, there is an index of topic headings starting on page 97.

Chapter 1: How your firm works

Just as a politician's only job is to get re-elected (think about it, even if that's all they do, they keep their job), I reveal what YOUR job actually is. There is also a simple explanation of why companies hire your firm. Finally, I have provided an overview of the different levels in the firm along with their basic responsibilities to give you a perspective on where you fit, what to focus on during your first year, and what you can expect as you progress through the firm.

Chapter 2: Clothing

You will likely be buying a whole new wardrobe for your new job. Assuming you are on a budget, I have provided you with guidance to give you the best long-term value for your money.

Chapter 3: Managing your work

The chapter is the main focus of the book. It discusses the most basic knowledge and skills you will need to navigate your first year. It will also help you develop the habits you will need to develop yourself professionally and set yourself up for long-term success.

Chapter 4: Exceeding expectations

"Exceeding expectations" is a term used by pretty much everyone in the industry, but relatively few people provide much practical guidance as to how to actually do it. This chapter is my answer, based on 25 years of almost daily reflection on the topic.

Chapter 5: Rules

I firmly believe that there are absolute truths in the business world. This is my take on the most important ones.

Your turn

To get the most effective use of this book, you need to make it your own. As you come across things you want to remember that are not covered in this book, or want a place to record lessons learned, write them down. It will help you succeed, and will help you become a better counselor and leader.

Chapter 1: How your firm works

Professional services firms started out as providers of very specific services (in the case of Public Accounting firms, independent audit and tax services). In the delivery of these services, a small group of people – the first Partners – formed a firm, and hired people to work under them, basically as apprentices, to learn the business. Fast-forward to today, and these firms are multi-billion dollar global organizations that provide a vast array of professional services, have developed detailed standards and processes, and have extensive training programs to ensure that their entire organization delivers consistent quality work products. And yet, they still operate on that same apprenticeship model.

Much of the work you do will be in relatively small teams, and your experience and development will be significantly dependent on the individuals immediately around you. It is crucial that you understand some basics about how your firm actually interacts with clients, and more importantly at this stage of your career, how you relate to and interact with the people in your office and in your practice.

Your actual job (it's not about being right)

If you ask a random person at your firm to tell you what their job is, they will likely start describing a series of tasks or projects. They are focused on the wrong thing. They are describing what they DO, not what makes them successful. If you ascribe to their view, you run the real risk of working very hard and not seeing the career results you would like to see.

Your actual job is to gain the trust of the people for and with whom you work. How you go about doing this certainly has a lot to do with performing well at the various tasks and projects on which you work, but it involves so much more than just executing your work. Put simply, you will get promoted because people trust you to deliver quality work, communicate well, meet deadlines, work well in teams, innovate, have

How Your Firm Works

5

integrity, and I could keep writing this list for a couple of pages. The point is, it is not enough for you to do all of these things – the people for whom you work have to **trust** that you will do them.

> A few years ago I was running a project and needed an additional staff person on my team. The only individual available was highly intelligent, but not viewed as a high performer, and was probably about four months from being terminated. We went out to lunch on his first day on my project to discuss the work and my expectations of him. He was extremely frustrated with his work experience to date, and started describing several situations where he had run-ins with his Seniors and Managers. His entire focus was on the fact that, in each situation, he believed that he was correct about an issue or approach, and in a couple of situations, I could see (at least based on his version of the facts) where he may have had a legitimate point.
>
> He explained that in a couple of situations he had taken his issue directly to the Manager (over the head of his Senior). When I asked him why, his response was, basically, "I was right." I spent the next 15 minutes or so talking to him about teamwork and the need for trust, particularly in small teams. When I asked him how he thought it made his Seniors feel when he took an issue over their heads, it was like a light bulb went off in his head, and he suddenly understood what I had been talking about for the last 15 minutes.
>
> He went on to perform very well on my project, and got very high marks from the Senior on the job. While he did leave the firm about a year later, it was because he got a great opportunity, not because he was asked to leave.

Responsibility for gaining trust is on the individual gaining it (YOU), not the people bestowing it. Remember, if you don't gain their trust, it may slightly negatively impact them, but it hurts you a LOT.

Chapter 1: How your firm works

What clients pay for

Your clients pay a lot of money for your services, and on the surface, most of those services are relatively straight-forward; you are conducting an external audit, executing an internal audit project, assisting in the re-design of business processes associated with the implementation of a new accounting software package, preparing a set of tax returns, or performing some other service with a well-defined scope and set of deliverables.

They could hire any one of dozens of firms, many of which may be significantly less expensive, to perform these tasks. So why have they chosen your firm? Whether it is explicitly stated or not, they have hired you, in part, to gain access to your firm – your people, your processes, your knowledge base and your experience. While you certainly have to deliver on the stated objectives of a given project, you are also expected to identify problems and develop solutions to those problems. Some of those issues will arise in the context of the particular project for which you are engaged, but you cannot limit yourself to thinking only of the things that are right in front of you.

During the course of ANY project, you will be exposed to other aspects of your client organization. It is your job to keep your eyes and ears open to challenges your client is facing, bring those to the attention of your Seniors and project executives, and assist in developing solutions, or approaches to developing solutions relative to those challenges.

> Your clients are paying you to identify and help resolve problems. Your clients' problems do not follow a nice, neat schedule. When your client has a problem, you need to view it as YOUR problem as well, and be willing to help resolve it on THEIR timetable. When your client has a problem that arises at 5:00pm on a Friday, you can either think "darn – there goes my weekend," or you can think "here is a great opportunity for my client to say 'wow, I'm glad I hired them!'"

Chapter 1: How your firm works

Do not just keep your head down and execute the specific tasks assigned to you – your client could have hired anyone to do that. Your client made a conscious decision to hire your firm – your job is to make that look like a really smart decision.

Levels and basic responsibilities

Accounting firms have been around for a long time. Their basic organization, levels and related support structures are well-established and effective... to deliver basic Audit and Tax services. Most consulting organizations are relatively new, Many of the current consulting service models have only existed since the late 90's, and the adoption of Sarbanes-Oxley and the service needs that flowed from it led to significant changes again only about five years later.

> Consulting in major accounting firms started to become a significant factor in the 1970's and 1980's. These consulting groups, however, focused on very different services when compared to today's consulting groups. The early groups had a major focus on computer programming, and then process outsourcing. Even before some of these practices became separate legal entities, firms had already begun to develop groups that delivered additional consulting services in the gaps that were outside the core competency of their official Consulting practices. These groups evolved and became, or were incorporated into, today's accounting firm consulting organizations.

Why is this important? One major result of these circumstances is that Public Accounting firms, which are still very audit- and tax-centric, have staff development, training programs and people models which are very mature when it comes to teaching their people to deliver on the tasks related to external audits and tax services. However, when it comes to identifying and helping resolve the wide variety of problems every company has to deal with on a daily basis (remember "What clients pay

Chapter 1: How your firm works

for?") the staff development and training programs are not nearly as mature. In addition, the people models don't necessarily reflect the way that these more consultative activities are identified and delivered.

Most firms have development models that are, in essence, lists of competencies expected from each level of professional employee. While these can be helpful, I have always found them to be lacking in providing guidance to me and my counselees when helping explain how to progress in the firm.

In large part, because of the greater diversity of services provided, professional services organizations have become much more fluid; you may often find yourself, as a Staff-level employee, reporting directly to a Director, or even to a Partner, on a particular project.

So how, then, are you supposed to manage your progression through the firm?

Most people, if they are honest with you, just try to deliver high-quality work, and look for opportunities to take on tasks they see their superiors performing. They may be told that they need to "exceed client expectations," or "see the big picture," to reach the next level – this is about as helpful as having a golf instructor tell you to "just hit the ball onto the green."

There are two basic groups of competencies that you will develop throughout your career; technical skills and management skills. The technical skills you need to develop are widely varied, and depend almost totally on your practice and the client base you serve. The management skills, on the other hand, are almost universal. More importantly, **your ability to get promoted through the firm is much more heavily influenced by your ability to master and demonstrate competencies in this area**.

Chapter 1: How your firm works

Virtually all firms have the same basic personnel structure, with the following levels:

Title	Duration	Comments
Staff (or Associate)	2-3 years	This is the entry level into the firm. All inexperienced hires start at this level.
Senior (or In-Charge)	2-4 years	Some firms have a Supervisor level between Senior and Manager. For the purpose of this discussion you should consider this role to be basically identical to a very strong Senior. Seniors are often the highest level resource performing day-to-day work at their clients.
Manager	2-4 years	This is the most difficult role in the firm, as the primary responsibilities for this position are split pretty evenly between tactical and strategic.
Senior Manager (or Director)	4+ years	Some firms have both of these levels. For the purpose of this discussion, you should consider this role to be similar for both titles. Most firms will not promote someone to this level unless the Partners believe that the individual has the potential to become a Partner.
Partner	n/a	These are the owners of the firm. The mindset and commitment level required of this position are completely different from that which is required at any other level. Having said that, there is a hierarchy among Partners – almost all have people they have to report to, just like you.

Chapter 1: How your firm works

The management competencies and skills needed to succeed at each of these levels can be grouped into five areas, each of which is associated with the levels listed above; (1) Your Work, (2) Others, (3) Engagements, (4) Clients and (5) The Firm. Understand these, and you have a basic understanding of what it actually means to "be" each of those levels. This book is primarily focused on the management competencies required to succeed in your first year – managing your work.

The following table illustrates the primary ● , secondary ◒ , and tertiary ○ management competencies for each level in the firm.

	Staff	Senior	Manager	Director	Partner
Your Work	●	◒	○	○	○
Others	◒	●	◒	○	○
Engagements	○	◒	●	◒	○
Clients		○	◒	●	◒
The Firm			○	◒	●

As you gain an understanding of the basic responsibilities of each level in the organization, there is one critical consideration that may not be clearly explained to you:

You need to deliver on the primary responsibilities at your level to keep your job. You need to deliver on the primary responsibilities at the level above you to get promoted. In other words, you will not get promoted to Senior by being a great Staff; you will get promoted to Senior by demonstrating the ability to perform the primary responsibilities of a Senior. The same applies to each promotion level.

Chapter 1: How your firm works

Managing your work

Your first responsibility is to learn how to manage, essentially, yourself. Some of it is really basic, like showing up for work every day, mastering your firm's time and expense entry system (and completing these on time, every time!) and learning how to manage voicemail and email.

Some of your responsibilities are a little more complex (and conceptually new), like learning how to document your work, perform effective self-review, work within the construct of a budget, and write concisely and effectively (this is harder than it sounds – you will likely have to unlearn some of the things you have learned in school).

Lastly, you will have to learn some more esoteric skills, like how to interact effectively with peers, superiors and clients, how to establish yourself as professionally dependable, and how to receive feedback and respond to it appropriately.

Chapter 3: Managing Your Work is dedicated to these topics.

Managing others

Maybe for the first time in your life, you are really responsible for managing other people – teaching them, making them productive, developing them, and most importantly, being accountable for their performance. This is the point in your career where you will first start to experience the simple truth that you are only as successful as the people underneath you.

You will need to develop the ability to manage complex budgets, delegate effectively, and review the work of others and provide meaningful feedback. As if that were not enough, you will need to start to learn how to effectively manage upward – that is, manage the time of the Managers, Senior Managers and Partners for whom you work.

Chapter 1: How your firm works

Managing others is the primary success factor for Seniors, who are, in many ways, the backbone of your firm. They are the face of the firm to most client personnel, and have primary responsibility for delivering the bulk of the work. Even for documents and other work initially created by others, they are fully responsible for the quality of everything produced by their team.

The plus side of this role is that your firm recognizes this, and you will get full credit for the production of your entire team, not just the work products you produce yourself.

Managing engagements

Managing the work of others is very tactical, while the next level, managing engagements, is a lot more strategic in nature. For this reason, the promotion from Senior to Manager is one of the most difficult transitions in your firm.

Managing individual projects and engagements does consist of a lot of tactical responsibilities, like managing WIPs (if you don't know what WIPs are, see the box at the end of this section), scheduling and planning engagements (which often consist of multiple projects that you will need to schedule and plan), billing your clients, creating final deliverables and completing other related administrative tasks. The most challenging (and more interesting) aspect of these tactical activities is that they will nearly always directly impact the client personnel who hired you – they will receive and pay your bills, receive and often present your reports, and will be directly impacted by your ability to coordinate scheduling with other client personnel. This means that when you are performing these tasks, you must always keep in mind the broader implications of what you are producing, how you are communicating it, etc.

As an example, billing may seem like a pretty straight-forward (tactical) activity. You have performed work, and you need to generate a bill to send to your client so that your firm can get paid. In almost all cases, this does NOT mean you just figure out what you (or even your firm) think the client owes you and send a bill for that amount. This is a great recipe for upsetting clients.

In most cases, you should be regularly meeting with your primary client contact (if you don't know who that is, it's probably the person who approves your bills for payment) and discussing your progress and related fees and expenses they should expect on their next billing, including tracking your billing against the total fees quoted at the beginning of the engagement. The discussion should also include anticipated future fees and expenses, which will make future meetings more productive.

Other primary responsibilities related to managing engagements include managing project scope, solving technical problems and identifying internal process improvements, communicating regularly with client management and presenting the results of your work.

Chapter 1: How your firm works

What are WIPs? At a VERY high level...

A WIP, or Work In Process is the tool your firm uses to track fees, expenses, write-offs, fee reserves and billings related to client work. Every time you post an hour to a client code in your time reporting system, that hour gets posted, at your internal billing rate, to that job's WIP. Every time you post an expense to a client code, that expense amount gets posted to that job's WIP.

Each job has a recovery percentage assigned to it, which is basically a built-in write-off, and this percentage is applied to each hour posted to that WIP (if your rate is $200/hour and your job is set up with a 60% recovery rate, every time you post an hour, $200 in fees and an immediate $80 reserve are posted to that WIP, for an unbilled balance of $120). Client billings are applied to the WIP when processed, and if there is an unbilled balance at the end of a project, an unplanned write-off must be processed.

All you need to know at this stage is that unplanned write-offs are very, very bad. People can, and do, get fired for large unplanned write-offs.

Managing clients

Clients hire your firm for a variety of reasons. Your services may be required to fulfill a regulatory requirement, to provide a vital operational function, or to solve a specific problem. The simple fact is that there are several firms who could provide these services; the goal of effective client management is to ensure that they hire YOU.

Your firm spends a lot of time and effort developing slides, pamphlets and other marketing and proposal materials that demonstrate the unique competencies and knowledge that should compel clients and prospective clients to hire you over your competition. Competing firms do this as well. While each firm truly believes it is unique and special, when viewed from the outside, the difference between any two of the firms is usually negligible. With the exception of price, on which basis many clients will ultimately make their decision to hire a particular firm, there is one HUGE differentiating factor in the pursuit of clients – Trust. It is a simple fact of life that people tend to do business with people they trust. Effective client management is mostly about building that trust.

Effective client management requires you to think like your client – you need to be able to view every situation, including your relationship with them, from their point of view. If you can consistently demonstrate this ability, you have the basis for building a trust-based relationship. Client management activities include:

- Managing the overall planning, delivery and execution of all services provided to a client organization
- Developing and nurturing relationships with key client executives
- Identifying needs at current clients where your group, or other service areas in your firm can provide solutions
- Networking in industry and technical professional organizations
- Identifying and pursuing opportunities at prospective clients

The ultimate goals for an individual at this level in your organization are to build a book of business and to demonstrate the ability to consistently grow revenue at existing clients, and effectively pursue and acquire new clients for the firm.

Chapter 1: How your firm works

Managing the firm

Managing the firm means running a business. While other management responsibilities are focused on the pursuit of, and delivery of service to clients, managing the firm basically involves making sure that all of that client activity results in profit, both now and into the future. Effective management of the firm also requires regular growth – without growth, your firm cannot reasonably add Partners, and it will die.

Some of the key areas of focus at this level include:

- People planning and execution
- Marketing/Sales planning
- Practice profitability
- Establishing a market presence
- Negotiating with clients
- Closing opportunities

Partners have a unique position within your firm. They are not simply the people at the top of your organizational charts – they are the owners of the firm. Every client billing, every expense, every paycheck, every write-off, every single dollar that flows through your firm directly impacts their personal financial well-being. The day you make Partner, your entire perspective about your firm will be completely altered.

Every single thing your firm does is ultimately the responsibility of your Partners. While public companies have to ultimately answer to shareholders, your Partners, collectively, ARE your shareholders. Keep this in mind when trying to understand why they make some of the decisions they do – it will help you understand them better.

Chapter 2: Clothing

Why a whole chapter on clothing? There are several reasons actually:

- This is one of the single biggest (from a monetary standpoint) investments you will make towards your first year of employment.
- For many of you, this is the first time you will need to establish a professional wardrobe – what was perfectly acceptable in college, even if you dressed well, is likely not ideal for your new environment.
- How you present yourself will have a huge impact on how you are viewed by your bosses and peers.
- Most importantly, this is the area where I have provided the most advice to first-year professionals.

The advice provided here is conservative – most Partners, clients and others who can have the greatest influence on your success or failure will, regardless of how "unfair" it may be, make preliminary judgements about you based on how you present yourself. Present yourself as a professional, and you are much more likely to be accepted as one. Take a look around, and with relatively few exceptions, you will notice that business executives dress conservatively.

The advice provided here is not absolute – there are many professionals who may have different opinions on certain aspects. In addition, there are parts of the world where the norm for business dress is unique (e.g., Hawaii, Bermuda) and requires adjustments from what is contained in this chapter. However, this is the advice I have been giving staff people for years - if you came to me for clothing advice, this is exactly what I would tell you.

Obviously, if any of the advice here is contrary to your religeous beliefs or customs, please disregard it.

Chapter 2: Clothing

Dressing to fit in

The remainder of this chapter provides advice that is applicable in most work environments – but not all. I previously mentioned that there are locations where the standard dress code is unique, and you will need to adjust the advice here to reflect that standard. Keeping in mind that you should be following the lead of your superiors, not necessarily your peers when it comes to dress, take a look at the executives in your organization and build your wardrobe accordingly.

In addition, even working in more "formal" cities like New York, certain of your clients may have dress codes that are more casual than the standard in your office environment. In general, most professional services organizations will encourage their staff to follow their clients' dress standard when they are at client locations. It not only helps the client accept you, but it can be very uncomfortable when you are clearly more formally dressed then EVERYONE around you.

Before you visit a client location for the first time, ask your Senior or Manager about the dress code. This is particularly important if your client location is out of town (as you will be stuck with what you pack).

> A few years ago, while working in New York, I had a technology client in Vermont. The project was several months long, and when we first showed up we were dressed in our standard attire, suits, long-sleeved dress shirts and the like. It was not uncomfortable, but we got some good-natured ribbing from the client (the first time I met the CEO he walked into a meeting in long shorts, a tee shirt and flip flops). About two months into the project, we decided as a team to dress in more client-appropriate attire. When we walked in the door for our next meeting in our sneakers, jeans and hoodies, 30 client personnel immediately jumped to their feet and gave us a thunderous 30-second standing ovation. Lesson learned.

Chapter 2: Clothing

Dressing for work (men)

Your business clothing is a commodity. You should shop for and buy it accordingly.

Suits

As you prepare to start your new job, you are going to be tempted to buy dress pants and a couple of sport coats, and wear those every day. While this is perfectly acceptable, I would strongly recommend you make an investment up front and buy at least three suits instead. There are several reasons for this, but primarily:

1. It's easier: If you build the right wardrobe, pretty much any shirt goes with any suit, and your jacket will always go well with your pants.
2. It looks better: While it's easy to make fun of some executives' sense of "style", take a look around. This is how the majority of senior executives dress. You want to be looked at as a serious professional, and this is an easy way to give yourself a head start in that area.
3. If the occasion comes up where you need to be in a suit, *you are already in one*. Just add a tie and you are good to go.

Don't EVER pay full price for a suit. Unless you are living under a rock, you are well aware of several suit sales going on pretty much any time. My personal recommendation is Brooks Brothers outlet stores, although there are several other completely acceptable options. One trick you can use to extend the useful life of a suit is to buy two pairs of pants to go with the suit jacket (this is easy at many stores which actually sell them seperately). Ask anyone who has worn suits for any period of time – the pants wear out or just get damaged a lot faster than the jackets, so you may be able to effectively double the life of your suit this way. If you do take this approach, make sure you rotate the pants such that you wear them equally with the jacket (think about it - you will be wearing the pants all day long each day, while the jacket will spend much of its time hanging up somewhere).

Buy blue and grey (and shades thereof) suits. If you want to get crazy, something like a dark olive color works as well. Finally, whatever you do, don't buy cheap suits – they look it.

> Cuffs or no cuffs?
>
> Generally speaking, pleated pants tend to look better with cuffs and straight leg pants tend to look better without cuffs (or so I'm told – all of my suit pants have cuffs, regardless). In addition, cuffs are more of an American thing, while European style tends to avoid cuffs. In my opinion, it's simple – look around your office or downtown area and see what your bosses or other executives have – do the same.

Shoes and belts

Shoes take more of a beating than any other piece of clothing. You could take one of two basic approaches here; either buy good (leather-soled always!) shoes and take care of them, or buy cheap shoes and replace them more often. There is actually only one correct answer – buy the better shoes.

1. It's less expensive overall: If you take good care of them, a high-quality pair of shoes can last eight-ten years, and even with regular maintenance, your overall cost will be lower than buying new, cheaper shoes every year or two.
2. They will look better: With good shoes, the vast majority of the wear and tear on your shoes is in the soles; cheaper shoes wear down a lot faster, and will look worn much sooner, especially on the part of the shoe everyone else can see.

3. It's a lot better for your feet: You will be on your feet a lot in the office, walking around at clients, and walking (or running) through airports, and your feet will not appreciate spending 16-hour days in cheap shoes.

A "good" pair of shoes should cost you around $200. Your shoes should be all leather, including leather soles. Don't buy the pair that "Looks just the same! But costs only $100! And maybe even has much more comfortable, rubber soles!" They do NOT look just the same, and will look even worse after a very short period of time.

I have almost exclusively purchased Johnston & Murphy shoes my entire career, and the only other viable option for me is Allen Edmunds. This is just my personal experience, but every other shoe I have purchased has worn out in a year or two at the most, and most of them have looked a bit worn faster than that.

You need at least two pairs of shoes. You should generally not wear the same pair of shoes two days in a row, as good dress shoes need a break. If you wear leather shoes every day, the sweat from your feet will eat away the leather much faster than if you give them a day off (with shoe trees) so that they can fully dry before you wear them again. I would suggest having three pairs, which allows for one pair to be with the shoe-repair guy for a couple of days when needed.

After you buy your shoes, and before you wear them even once, take them to a shoe repair shop and have them put taps on the heels and attach rubber half-soles (this should run you $30-$40). You can keep the half-soles until the rubber wears out at the ball of your foot, but then you need to replace them immediately. The taps should last 2-3 months, depending on how hard you walk, and you should replace them as soon as they wear out. If you let the taps go without replacing them soon enough, you will immediately start to wear out the rubber part of

Clothing

23

your heels, which make it harder to attach taps (which should be less than $5).

If you have failed to heed this advice and you wear out the rubber heel (and by the way, when you start to really wear out the heel, your shoes will look shabby to anyone who is paying attention) or the leather sole, take them to a shoe repair shop and have them do a full sole replacement. This will cost you $60-$80, but is obviously much cheaper than a new pair of shoes.

Buy black shoes. They go with everything (including your jeans – see tip 8 in the Travel basics section of Chapter 3) and are always in style. If you want some variety, your third pair of shoes can be dark burgundy. Burgundy shoes go well with any of your blue suits. Do not buy brown shoes, as they will require a whole new complement of suits, and unless your parents are made of money (and are willing to share it with you), you really don't want to spend all of your money on clothing.

Buy a belt for each pair of shoes (black for black, burgundy for burgundy), and just get plain, nice dress belts – buy fancy boxers if you need to express yourself with your clothing. While you can buy your belts the same place you buy your shoes, I have actually had much more success over the years with plain Coach belts. In my experience they just last a LOT longer.

If your shoes don't come with shoe trees, buy them and use them. Also buy three extra pairs of shoelaces for each color of shoes. Keep one in your office, one at home, and one in your computer bag.

Suspenders and vests

I recommend against both.

Chapter 2: Clothing

Shirts and ties

Unlike suits and shoes and belts, shirts are where you should feel free to express yourself. HA! Not really. You are going to be boring (professional) here as well.

You are going to need at least 12 shirts (long sleeves only!), and I recommend around 20. You can walk into a high-end retailer and pay upwards of $90 per shirt – please don't do this. Brooks Brothers outlets have them for about $50 per shirt, and if you find a sale, as little as $40. You can find sales at Jos A Bank that put you more in the $35 range. Land's End usually has a few sales per year where you can get them around $35 as well. There are many other workable options here, but the key is to get very basic colors and patterns – bright colors = bad; muted colors = good.

> There was a time, about 25 years ago, when some companies and firms all but required plain white shirts and nothing else (I actually witnessed a fellow first-year associate being sent home one day to change out of his blue shirt and into a white one). Thankfully those days are gone. I think I have two white shirts left in my closet.

I am a huge fan of the non-iron shirts. Even if they cost a bit more (and they don't always), they more than pay for themselves in MUCH lower maintenance cost. Consider the fact that if a shirt lasts 40 wears and you take it to the cleaner each time, you are going to spend at least $40 for cleaning over the life of that shirt (If you are planning instead on ironing your own shirts, God bless you). The key with non-iron shirts is to remove them from the dryer IMMEDIATELY after they are dry and hang them up. They will hold their crease.

Chapter 2: Clothing

There are three basic styles of shirt – button-down collars, straight collars and french cuffs (which also have straight collars):

Button-down collars – This is the most popular style of shirt, and is what I would recommend you purchase for the majority of your shirts. I am of the opinion that they look better (neater) than straight collars when worn without ties. Although you should not plan to wear them with ties, in an emergency you can get away with it.

Straight collars – If your job (e.g., your one, large client) requires you to wear a tie pretty much every day, this will likely be your best option. As implied above, they can also be worn without ties in a business casual setting. You will need to wear collar stays with these shirts – always – every time - without exception. If you don't, and your collar starts to stray, it just looks bad. Trust me. Plastic collar stays (you will get a pair in the shirt when you purchase it) actually work, although the metal ones are much more durable. Keep at least one pair of collar stays in your computer bag.

French cuffs – This is about a stylish as you should expect to get – ever. French cuff shirts look great, but will need cuff links (obviously) and this just adds to the cost of your wardrobe.

Assuming you don't need to wear a tie every day, you will still need at least five ties. Do not use ties to express yourself. Buy basic stripes (diagonal!) and patterns, and don't go skinny or cheap. Having said that, don't ever pay full price – find a sale and buy a few good ties for $20-30 apiece.

Socks and undershirts

Some people choose to purchase very nice and relatively expensive socks. One such individual may have 20-30 pairs of socks, each pair at least slightly different from the next. They may be arranged meticulously in a sock drawer, likely based on which suit(s) they go with. Assuming they are business-appropriate (no stripes, no bright colors, etc), that is a perfectly acceptable choice. And in my opinion a total pain in the butt. Try packing for a week-long trip at the last minute, mostly in the dark so as not to disturb your spouse/roommate any more than necessary, and perfectly coordinate five selections from 20 different sock options to go with the two suits (which you have also grabbed in the dark). That blue pair of socks you accidentally grabbed will not be acceptable with the grey and olive suits you just packed.

My solution is quite simple. I buy plain black socks, and I buy them in bulk (10-12 pairs at a time). The advantages are easy to explain:

1. All the socks are black. Black socks go with all black and burgundy shoes, and all blue, grey and olive suits (and therefore, everything in my closet)
2. All of the socks are essentially identical. There is no need to spend any time whatsoever selecting socks.
3. Because all of the socks are identical, there are no set pairs. If you have individual pairs of socks, when you get a hole in one, both socks get thrown out. In my system, when a sock wears out, I throw it out and it's former partner waits for another single sock to form a new pair (this also makes laundry just a bit easier).

Undershirts are also easy, and in my opinion, not optional (see the story in the outlined box below). An undershirt tends to be more comfortable against your skin (even in extreme, muggy heat) than a dress shirt, and by keeping your much more expensive dress shirt away from your skin, it will last longer.

Your three basic undershirt choices are tanktops, crew necks and v-necks. Tanktops are out because they don't cover your armpits, which is the primary source of that sweat that will quickly ruin a dress shirt.

Clothing

Chapter 2: Clothing

Crew-neck or v-neck undershirts are both good options. Buy white undershirts, as they will not show through any of your shirts.

Note: If you have chest hair that a v-neck shirt will show off, crew necks may be a better option for you.

> Undershirts: Not just for old men.
>
> Early in my career, I was in a one-on-one meeting with one of the employees at a client. At one point during the meeting, he leaned back in his chair and put his hands behind his head, pulling his shirt slightly apart and showing me, through the gap where he missed a button, a hairy belly button area. I literally bought undershirts on the way home that day and have worn them every single work day since.

Extra clothing in the office

Find a place to keep an extra shirt and a belt in the office. The shirt, because you don't want to have to wear a coffee- or food-stained shirt all day if you don't have to. The belt, because trust me, you will forget to put on a belt every so often.

Chapter 2: Clothing

Business casual

With the exception of a few companies in the financial district of New York City, the overwhelming majority of companies, including your firm, dress business casual on a daily basis.

Let's first discuss what business casual at your firm is not:

- Jeans, dockers or anything but dress pants or suits
- Polo shirts, or anything but LONG-SLEEVED dress shirts
- Sneakers, boat shoes, cool boots or anything but dress shoes

In other words, dress pants or suits, long-sleeved dress shirts and dress shoes. Business casual simply means "no tie."

Business casual on steroids: Jeans Day

Your office may use "Jeans Day" to support a worthy cause. You donate five or ten dollars, and you get to wear jeans into the office on a particular day (assuming you have no client meetings). Awesome. Donate the money, and dress the way you always do.

If you haven't figured out why...

What if a last-minute meeting comes up in the middle of Jeans Day, and you have the opportunity to go, and maybe meet an important person at a client or potential client, and ride in a car with a Partner and Director, preparing for the meeting on the way to the client, and work with them directly after the meeting on something big and important and...oooooh. Too bad you are in jeans – the first year Staff who sits next to you is in a suit. He gets to go instead. Be nice to that guy, he will eventually be your boss.

Chapter 2: Clothing

Dressing for work (women)

First, let us start off by stating that most women probably do not need as much help as most men do when it comes to building their professional wardrobe. Most women read fashion magazines of one type or another, shop for clothing more often than do men and in general have a more developed sense of style. That being said, following is a high level overview of what women should consider when entering the corporate world. While it may not be how you would choose to dress, it should be the way you do outfit yourself in the workplace. After all, you are there to work, learn and further develop your career and the last thing you want to have happen is to be held back because your personal style is considered immature, unflattering or simply unprofessional.

Before even getting into the specifics on dress, one of the most important things to remember is to wear clothes you can work in without being in pain (no too-tight pants or skirts, blouses that gap between the buttonholes, or conversely items so loose that you need to constantly hike them up to avoid losing them). Likewise, avoid clothing that you have to continually tug on or readjust because the garments you are wearing are ill-fitting. Fit is extremely important. You want to be professional on the job but you also want to feel comfortable enough so that you can work without worrying about what your clothing is doing.

Successful women adhere to their company's dress code. While there may be more leeway regarding the professional female dress code vs. that of their male counterparts, successful women understand that there are certain standards of dress that should be followed, even when there is not a specific formal dress policy. Your ultimate goal in dress is to present a professional and competent image, and the style, color and fit of your wardrobe can provide confidence to those for whom you will work that you are concerned about your career and the image of the firm.

Even with a formal dress code, the best indication as to how you should dress is to see what your female Manager or Partner wears. How many times does she wear skirt suits vs. pantsuits? Does she wear dresses? What kinds of shoes does she wear and how does she excessorize her outfit?

If for some implausible reason there is no higher level female you work with to emulate, then it is best to take a look at what your male Manager and Partner are wearing and dress accordingly. If they are wearing suits and ties on a daily basis then you should probably be wearing matched pantsuits and skirt suits. You need to be as business formal as they are so that you look like one of the team.

Clothing Career Killers

As unfair as it may seem, wearing certain fashion items can potentially inflict permanent damage on your career or at least your career in your current organization. Hopefully it goes without saying, but there are a few basic rules regarding what not to wear. There will be some more detail below, but in general, avoid wearing the following while at work:

Anything too suggestive – this means see-through, ultra-short, slit too high, cut too low.

Anything too casual – avoid wearing jeans, t-shirts, sneakers, sweatshirts, etc.

Anything too messy – any clothes that are wrinkled, dirty, baggy or otherwise ill-fitting.

Anything too bright or shiny – no metalic color blouses or shoes, excessive use of bright colors and crazy patterns.

Chapter 2: Clothing

Overview

Women have the option of a dress or skirt or pants. Any of these options are in all probability acceptable, provided that the choice is well tailored and looks professional. Again, however, it is a good idea to observe what your Manager or Partner wears when visiting a client and take your cue from her.

Try and buy the right clothes as you start out. While it may be hard on your current budget, spend a bit more money where you can to buy high quality clothing. After all, you will likely be wearing these items all day, several times a month and you want something that is going to last, will look good on you, and will make you feel good about yourself. Part of succeeding is having confidence in your abilities, and clothes that contribute positively to your self-esteem will go a long way in helping you display that confidence.

Pants

All pants need to be well-tailored, with lengths appropriate to the height of your shoes. While pleated pants are likely somewhat more professional looking, there are certainly many flat front pants that look equally as good if they are well-made from good fabrics such as merino wool, a merino wool and cashmere blend, linen, or a linen and silk blend, depending on the cut of suit and time of year. It is best to stick with the neutral colors – black, gray, and navy. A subtle pinstripe is also another respectable option.

If you do not already own one, it is probably a wise idea to purchase a tailored pantsuit or two. You may have to make a presentation to a client or group at some point and a suit will likely work best. Because women's wear tends to change styles or design more frequently than that of men, you should definitely buy something that is classic, as you do not want your "good" suit to be out of style when you need to use it the next year. Make sure the pants are tailored for the most businesslike appearance. For something that may be a significant financial investment, or even if it is not, look for pants and suits in those neutral colors – black, gray, and navy/dark blue are always safe choices.

Not all your pants need to come with matching jackets. Women can also wear tailored knit sweater and sweater sets, although these should be considered more business casual than formal business. More detail about tops follows. Also, a tailored jacket can be purchased separately and worn with either pants or a skirt.

Dresses and skirts

If you decide to wear a dress or skirt, opt for knee-length, or slightly above the knee over either mini- or maxi-skirts. The fashion in any particular year or season may dictate one of these variations but in general they are considered inappropriate and unprofessional for the office. Knee-length skirts and dresses are universally flattering. Also, avoid slits that are too high above the knee. They can make an otherwise professional skirt suddenly quite inappropriate.

There are various dress styles available; many are work appropriate. Some are less suitable for corporate business dress codes, but may be appropriate in a business casual setting. To make a dress more formal, pair it with a suit jacket or blazer. If you choose to wear a dress, it is best to look for a simple A-line dress with a knee length skirt and a conservative neckline. Solid color dresses or those with a small pattern are most fitting. This eliminates short hems on the bottom, spaghetti straps, plunging or sheer fabric necklines on top, and frills anywhere.

Clothing

Chapter 2: Clothing

Tops

This includes blouses, shirts and other possibilities. For men there is the long sleeve dress shirt. Women have other options available to them, with some being more appropriate than others. In any event, this is an area where you can show a little more color than what is suggested for pants, suits and skirts. Most women know the shades that look good on them. If not, ask your friends or someone you trust to help you identify those colors that look best with your skin tone and buy tops in those shades. They will make you and your suits look even better. Collared or simple shell tops work best under a jacket.

Women should always keep their shoulders and upper arms covered. This means no spaghetti straps, no sleeveless blouses and no tube or halter tops. While I cannot fathom any woman even thinking of wearing the latter two to work, there are probably quite a few who have considered wearing a sleeveless blouse or perhaps even a slightly frilly camisole underneath a tailored suit jacket. While either can look very nice and even quite professional while the jacket is on, the same cannot be said if you need to take your jacket off for any reason. A smartly cut and styled sleeveless blouse may look nice on occasion, but it will not work in more professional settings and is best avoided unless you know that your jacket will not be coming off until after you have left the office. The same applies to three-quarter sleeve blouses. They may look nice under a jacket; not quite so professional when uncovered. Button-up shirts, either long or short sleeved, and silk blouses should work well.

As noted previously, women can also chose to wear tailored knit sweater sets. As also mentioned, however, these are deemed more business casual than professional; again, take your lead from your female superiors. If you do decide to wear a sweater set make sure it is made of good material, meaning cashmere or at the least a wool cashmere blend, is free of pulls or nubs and is not faded or stretched out in any way. It is most likely easier to wear the tailored blouse just to be safe.

A note about weather

While the virtues of a well-tailored outfit made out of good material are unquestionable, wearing a heavy wool suit during a heat wave or on a business trip to an extremely warm climate can make you seem less competent. Smart women are sensible women, and this can be seen in the way they chose their clothing. This might mean switching to linen and cotton fabrics and changing over to a short sleeve blouse under your jacket.

Stockings

This is a topic that may be debatable, however, in my opinion it really is not. Women should wear sheer nylon stockings whenever they wear skirts or dresses. You may have beautifully toned legs, however, it may be considered less than professional to leave them uncovered. Flesh-toned is appropriate; find the shade that matches your natural color and stock up on that. All other colors should be avoided, although it may be acceptable to wear a sheer black nylon with a black skirt or dress during the winter months. Again, the best answer to this may be found in what female Managers and Partners are wearing. And whatever you do, always make sure that your stockings are run- and snag-free. Carry an extra pair in your handbag or briefcase for those times when you may need to make a quick change because of a run.

Shoes

Unlike men, women have an endless array of possibilities when it comes to shoes. Unfortunately, like men, they should probably stick with the classic work shoe, in this case, the pump. The most appropriate pump is one that is closed-toe leather with a ½ to 2 ½ inch heel. Know your limits. Heels should not be so high that you are in pain and/or you are teetering. Black is always in style, but other safe options include navy, burgundy, and brown, depending on what other colors you are wearing that day. It may be presumptuous, but I assume that most women know a "good" shoe from one that is not, and have a decent working knowledge about where and how to buy good shoes. Women are not as limited in where they can buy well-made leather shoes but most major department stores carry high end lines and are a good place to start.

One bit of advice women should take from men is that they should have taps and half-soles put on the bottom of their new shoes. It will help avoid early wear and tear and extend the life of the shoes. Also, make sure to keep your shoes clean, polished and scuff free. No matter how expensive, a scuffed shoe looks cheap.

It should go without saying, but I will mention it anyway – never wear "sexy" shoes to the office. While those four- or five-inch stiletto heels may be striking on a date or a night on the town, there is absolutely no place for them in the office or at a client. The same must be said for strappy heels. Likewise, do not wear sandals in the office; they show too much skin to be considered professional and can make a business outfit look frumpy.

There is also the issue of the open-toed pump. While this particular style may not be noted specifically in the office dress code it is wiser to avoid wearing them if at all possible. It is not that they are necessarily too revealing. It's just that they can look unprofessional, particularly if you are in proximity to other women who are wearing closed toed shoes.

Other footwear to avoid include the obvious – flip flops, sneakers and, in my opinion, boots. In bad winter weather it is certainly permissible, even sensible, to wear boots to the office. There is no reason to ruin a good pair of shoes. However, once you have arrived, make sure to exchange them for a pair of pumps.

Extra clothing in the office

Always keep an extra button-down or blouse (I suggest a white blouse; it will go with anything) in the office so you can make a quick change if you happen to spill something on yourself. Hopefully that will never happen, but it is always better to be prepared.

Accessories

A few well-chosen accessories can provide a bit of style to your wardrobe without making you stand out in a bad way. This is likely the easiest way to express yourself - within limits of course.

<u>Jewelry</u>

The easiest thing to remember about jewelry is that it should be largely forgettable to others. This means avoiding sparkly pieces that look great with evening wear, but not so much with a business suit. It also means to limit the amount of jewelry you put on. No one wants to know you are coming down the hall two minutes before you arrive because they can hear multiple bracelets jangling from your wrists. Similarly, avoid wearing multi-layered necklaces and rings on every finger. In general it is best to keep jewelry simple and unobtrusive, and that also includes earrings. The most appropriate options include posts and short (nowhere remotely near your shoulders) dangling or hoop earrings. And limit it to one pair. There is no need to wear two or more pairs of earrings to the office; leave those multiple ear piercings empty.

Chapter 2: Clothing

Finally, there may be some of you who have non-traditional piercings. This basically includes any piercing beyond the simple one hole in each earlobe. Whether it's in your nose, your lip, or your eyebrows, do yourself a huge favor and leave those for the weekend when you are not working.

<u>Purses and bags</u>

You may have a number of bags to carry when you visit a client site, so it is a good idea to invest in a small briefcase or business style tote. This is one area where I would spend the money to get a well-made, classic briefcase or tote, as it will be something you can use for years. Leather probably wears best, but if you cannot afford one, or are against using leather for any reason, there are well-made nylon or leather-like options available (e.g., Stella McCartney, Ivanka Trump, LAUREN by Ralph Lauren among others all make faux leather totes and bags). The key is to make sure the stitching is strong, the bag looks professional, and that it does not come with any embellishments (fringe, hanging logos, etc.). As with pants, skirts, and shoes, your best option is a neutral color such as black or port/burgundy.

You may also want or need to carry a purse. If that is the case, the guidelines are similar. You should opt for a black leather (or leather-like) structured shoulder bag with minimal hardware and relatively simple design. Slouchy bags tend to look somewhat sloppy and less than professional so save those for the weekend.

Chapter 2: Clothing

> A Simple Message on Logos
>
> While there are many designers who make beautiful clothing, shoes, bags etc., you do not want to look like a walking advertisement for any of them. A tote with a small designer label or shoes that may have a small logo on them is one thing, but walking in with designer names emblazoned all over you is not all that chic and frankly somewhat tacky. If it fits well and you've paired it appropriately with other items you are wearing, that is all that matters.

Make-up

While not technically an accessory, you can and should use make-up to highlight your good points. As with many other suggestions before, keep it simple. This essentially means to stick with the basics – foundation matching your natural skin tone, a natural-looking blush, lipstick shades close to your normal lip color and lightly applied eye make-up, which can include mascara and a natural shade of liner (avoid heavy black liners). You can use eye shadow, but avoid bold, bright colors and opt for lighter, less conspicuous shades. You want people to notice the work you do, not the amount of make-up on your face.

It is best to be as conservative with your nails as with the rest of your make-up. Keep your nails well-manicured, meaning relatively short and bare or with a natural, light color. No one wants to shake hands with someone whose fingers look as if they have been gnawed on or conversely, with someone who has such long nails that they look as if they might cause pain. In addition, excessively long nails may make computer use more difficult.

Chapter 2: Clothing

Perfume

You can wear it. However, make sure that the scent is subtle and not so overpowering that others can smell you before you've entered the room. You have probably at one point or another been around another woman (or man) who had on so heavy a scent and was practically bathed in his or her cologne that you felt as if you were choking. Do not be that person. Once again, you want co-workers and clients to remember you as the person who gets something done, and not the one who smells like a field of lilies.

Hair

Above all your hair should be neat and clean. Long or short, keep it out of your face. Highlighted or colored hair is fine, so long as those highlights or that color is not something unnatural. That means to avoid anything not typically found in nature – blue, pink, purple, etc.

Tattoos

This may seem trivial to mention, but there have been situations where individuals have been left back during trips to a new client or prospect because they had a tattoo that the Manager did not want to risk being seen by the client. The best idea is never to get one, particularly in an area – wrist, arm, ankle – where it will likely be seen by colleagues and clients. However, if you already have one you will need to cover it up as best as possible. This may mean longer sleeves on warmer days, fashion scarves worn around your neck, or potentially the use of body make-up in certain areas. If you absolutely have to get a tattoo, do yourself and your career a huge favor and have it put somewhere where there is absolutely no way anyone in the work environment will ever see it.

40

Chapter 2: Clothing

Business casual

"Business casual" does not mean "casual." For women in your firm, there is relatively little difference between business and business casual.

If you did not read it already, see the callout box at the end of the Dressing for work (men) section for a discussion of "Jeans Day."

Chapter 3: Managing your work

Managing your work will require you to learn how to manage your workday and master basic communication tools. These are addressed below as Logistics.

You will need to master the basic tasks your firm expects all employees to execute out of habit. It will also involve developing your ability to be an effective team member as well as your ability to lead small teams. These are addressed below as Basic skills.

Lastly, you will begin to develop your ability to manage your career, effectively interact with clients and develop relationships outside of your organization. These are addressed below as Development as a professional.

Logistics: Managing your workday

The most basic aspect of managing your work is managing your workday. What is your daily routine? Will you periodically work from home? If so, how will you manage that? How will you adjust to a professional environment?

The habits you form in your first few years will likely define your work style for the course of your career. Make sure you form good ones.

Arriving

Find out when your Senior(s) or Manager(s) typically arrive for work, and get in the habit of arriving a couple of minutes before they do. Your primary job is to execute tasks *at their direction*, and it will quickly frustrate them if you are not there first thing in the morning to take on tasks that they can assign to you.

When they (or you if they beat you in) arrive in the office, check in with them. This is a good way to connect with them and start building the trust you will need to move up in the firm. If they can rely on you being there when they need you, you have a good chance to end up with a lot more interesting and meaningful work than your peers.

24/7

You are in the professional services industry. Your clients are paying you to help them identify and solve problems, and due to the fact that they are paying upwards of $100/hour (and in some cases a LOT more) for the privilege of your time and effort, they expect a very high level of customer service. This does not end at 5:00 each day, and in a lot of cases, does not end at the end of the day on Friday, to be picked up again on Monday. Trust me; your Partners, Directors, Managers and Seniors are thinking about (and working for) their clients well into the evening and over weekends (at least the good ones are), and you would be well-served to do the same.

I am not saying that you have to spend all of your time working – you have to have a life. I am just saying that you cannot expect to roll in every day when the office opens and drop everything every day at 5:00. If you cannot reconcile yourself to this, *you have chosen the wrong place to start your career*. There are lots of good jobs for which you are likely qualified, and you should start looking for one.

Personal business

I have explained that you are in a job that will consume a large portion of your time; almost all of the people you work for will recognize this and will not have a problem if you periodically need to take care of personal business during working hours. Besides the obvious, here are a couple of guidelines you should follow:

- Do not conduct personal business in front of a client. If you are at a client location, find some privacy.

- If you have to deal with something that will take an inordinate amount of time, speak to your superior, and consider taking part of the day off so that you can concentrate on getting your personal issue resolved – you do not want to be a distraction to your co-workers.

- Track your personal time and make sure you account for it appropriately. You will gain a lot of credibility when your Senior questions you about your billable hours in a given day and you are able to demonstrate that you tracked your personal activity diligently – do not charge your client for the hour you spent on the phone with the cable guy.

Working from home

I am not a big fan of working from home, so in general I would discourage it. Too many good breaks, both large and small, occur because you happen to be in the right place at the right time, and the "right" place in those instances is never at home. You will also be encouraged by most of your superiors to spend as much time as you can at client offices.

However, I do recognize that working from home is desirable to many, and for people that work for me there is one simple rule: If you work from home, it needs to be a day when you are 100% chargeable (that means client-billable hours).

A Big 4 Partner for whom I have a tremendous amount of respect put it this way:

"You generally are asked to focus on three things; serving clients with quality, developing and mentoring others and building new business. None of these can be done as effectively from home as they can be at clients or in the office".

Chapter 3: Managing your work

Down time

There is always a Senior, Manager, Senior Manager or Partner working on something you can help with. If you find yourself in the position where you have no pressing responsibilities, walk the floor (or make some phone calls) and find out who is working on something urgent where you might be able to help. You are not being paid to be unproductive – ever.

Logistics: Communication

Your job requires strong communication skills. The habits you form with respect to management of your voicemail and email will have a large impact on how you manage, or mismanage your day-to-day activities. There are very few activities in your job that are not part of a team effort, and forming good habits here will go a long way towards you developing a reputation as a "go-to" player.

Communication, whether upwards or down, is always YOUR responsibility. Always err on the side of over-communicating.

Voicemail

Your voicemail, along with your email, is something you should monitor multiple times during the day (every one-two hours is a good rule of thumb). Your clients, superiors, and peers rightly expect that you will be checking these contact points every couple of hours. Bad things happen if you let one of these go unchecked for long periods of time (24 hours). Your firm may have a policy requiring you to check voicemail within specified periods – find out and adhere to it if they do.

On your first day in the office, sign into your voicemail and set up your greeting. I would suggest the following (assuming you work for XYZ Company and your name is Amanda Smith):

"You have reached the voicemail for Amanda Smith with XYZ Company. Please leave a message and I will get back to you at my earliest convenience. If you need to reach me immediately, please call my cell phone at XXX-XXX-XXXX."

THIS INCLUDES WHILE YOU ARE ON VACATION. When you do go on vacation, take advantage of the alternate greeting option/notification features and inform the persons leaving you voicemail or sending you email that you will be out of the office on vacation. It is in your best interest to check these a couple of times while you are out to make sure that you respond in a timely manner to any critical issues that come up. You may be on vacation, but your clients' issues do not take vacations.

When you do go on vacation, set up an alternate voicemail greeting. I would suggest the following:

"Hi, you have reached the voicemail for Amanda Smith with XYZ Company. I will be out of the office on vacation until Monday, August 16th, and will have limited access to voicemail. If you need to speak to someone immediately, please contact Mark Jones (obviously someone else on your team) at XXX-XXX-XXXX. Otherwise, please leave a message and I will get back to you when I return."

With the firms' focus on work/life balance, you may be encouraged to not check voicemail while on vacation. I would suggest that is not the best idea.

Managing your work

Chapter 3: Managing your work

Cell phones

You have one. Put it on your business card and in your email signature. Both your boss and your client will need to reach you at some odd times, or when you are simply out of the office. You are a professional, and your cell phone is now a part of your job, so...

Change your voicemail to something professional, like "Hi, you have reached Bob Smith's cell phone. Please leave a message and I will get back to you as soon as I can." Either your friends will understand why your message is no longer "Heeeeeyyyyy, it's Bob. I'm too drunk to answer the phone right now, so leave a message dude!" or you need to get new friends.

Dialing an international number

It's amazing how many people are completely clueless when it comes to dialing non-US phone numbers. It's pretty simple:

From a land line, dial 011 (the exit code for the US), then the country code, then the number. Virtually all international numbers are listed with their country code at the front.

From your cell phone, dial +, and then the country code and number.

If you need to dial internationally from outside of the US (say you are calling the US from the UK), you need to dial that country's exit code (which is 00 pretty much everywhere).

Don't forget that Canada and a lot of the Caribbean share the US country code (1), and you can call to or from there like you are calling within the US.

Chapter 3: Managing your work

Answering Your Phone

Whether you are answering your work phone or your cell phone (remember, your cell phone is now part of your job), the correct way to answer your phone is, "XYZ Company, Amanda Smith speaking," or some derivation thereof.

Practice it. Do it every time. Even on your cell phone. Even on the weekend.

Email

Email is the primary method people have of communicating with you – you are expected to keep current with your email, and this should come as no surprise to you. Your firm may have a policy regarding how often you check your email. Follow it. At the very least, you should try to check your email every couple of hours.

There are a few other things to keep in mind on this topic.

1. Email is permanent – take your time writing (and in many cases re-writing) your message. I have seen countless problems caused by carelessly written email messages.
2. Try to read your message from the point of view of the person or persons receiving it, and make sure they will receive the message you are trying to send.
3. Keep your email as short as possible without losing the meaning – if it needs to be longer, you should consider summarizing the contents of the message at the top.
4. There are very valid reasons to use email as the primary method of communication – usually when you want to create a documentation trail. In many situations however, it is much more efficient and effective to deliver your message in person or by phone (see Rule 4 in the final chapter of this book).

5. Pay close attention to who is copied on your email. Seriously consider whether it is appropriate before you hit the "reply all" button (hint – it is rarely appropriate).

6. In general, do not BCC (blind copy) people on your email. You run the risk of catching someone off guard if they do not realize that someone was copied on a message they received from you. BCC is generally used when you need to copy your superior, but do not want the recipient to know it. Do this only when absolutely necessary, as people will question your motivation for blind copying someone should they find out you did it.

7. At some point, you may notice that you are knee-deep in a virtual conversation over email. Many times it will be appropriate for you to just pick up the phone and call the other party.

Logistics: Travel

For many of you, work-related travel will be a regular occurrence. The sooner you develop a solid routine, the less stress you will experience. I have traveled a LOT over the course of my career (about 30-40% on average), and have gotten to the point where planning and packing for trips is very routine. Your approach to these topics may differ from mine, but this should provide you with a good place to start.

Travel basics

Coordinate your travel with the other members of your team – it will help immensely with car rentals and is generally better for bonding with your co-workers. If you are traveling solo and have to make your own plans, schedule your flights for early morning or evenings. Travel is part of your job, but your clients almost definitely do NOT intend to pay for your travel time, so unless you are doing billable work while on the plane or train or sitting in the airport, you should not be charging that time to your client. Find a way to make your travel time as productive as possible – even if all you are doing is cleaning up email.

With respect to packing for out of town assignments, here are a few tips:

1. Keep a small bag at home, into which you can fit a week's worth of clothing (carry on size only! Avoid checking a bag at almost ALL cost – you don't want to be the reason your whole team has to wait for checked bags when you land)
2. Have a complete set of TSA-friendly toiletries packed in a large Ziploc bag and keep it in the travel bag.
3. Guys, keep a spare black belt in the bag.
4. When folding dress pants/skirts, stack them and then roll them up. It will reduce wrinkling.
5. When folding shirts/blouses, stack them on top of each-other before you fold them. It will reduce wrinkling.
6. If you have to pack a suit jacket, put it in the plastic you get from the dry cleaners, fold it in half the long way, and then roll or fold it from the shoulders down.
7. When feasible, travel in business attire – it's one less suit to pack and you will look professional if you run into a client or your boss while traveling (it happens).
8. Take a pair of jeans. If you go out in the evening, you can just swap out your work pants or skirt for the jeans, and ditch your suit jacket. This keeps you from having to pack casual shoes, socks and shirts. It also reduces the risk of spilling something on your suit pants or skirt, which you may have to wear more than once during your trip.
9. If you have wrinkles in your clothing when you get to your destination, hang that day's clothes in the bathroom while you are showering – it will reduce the wrinkling a bit. You should

Managing your work

also consider touching up your clothing with the iron that should be in your hotel closet.

Keep a spare power supply for your PC and a spare phone charger in your computer bag. That way you don't have to remember them every time you travel.

Go bag

Keep a small bag in the office with toiletries and one or two days of clothing (the bare minimum is fine – you can re-wear your suit, belt and shoes in a pinch). There will be times when urgent, last minute travel comes up, and this simple thing can save you a lot of time and stress.

Passport

It's a good idea to get a passport if you don't already have one. They can take a month or more to get, and I have seen more than one staffing decision made because one of the individuals had a passport while another didn't.

Training

When you attend offsite training, do not forget that you are being PAID for attending and learning. If the training is not internal firm training, consider the possibility of putting together a presentation based on what you learned in your training. Talk to your Partner about presenting this at your next group meeting; this is an easy way to show initiative, and will help set you apart from your peers.

Chapter 3: Managing your work

Logistics: Dealing with different countries/cultures/languages

There is one basic rule here – respect the people with whom you are communicating. Many of our communication habits are subconsciously US-centric, and you should consider these when communicating outside of our borders. If you are not based in the US, understanding this section may help you in your communication with US-based co-workers and clients.

Speak (a little!) more slowly and clearly

The business world, almost universally, speaks English. For those whose native language is not English, they are doing you the favor of communicating in your language; do them the favor of speaking clearly.

Don't use colloquialisms/sarcasm/most humor

While most of the world speaks English, American terms (like "where the rubber meets the road" or "slam dunk") are not universally understood. In addition, while people from other countries may speak GREAT English (and in my experience, likely do), sarcasm and other humor are often not understood. They are doing you the favor of communicating in your language; do them the favor of speaking plainly.

> Attention, Americans! When you are speaking with people from the UK, keep in mind that THEY actually speak English (it's more their language than ours) – In the US we speak American English. These are not the same thing.

+1

In the US, while your phone number might actually be 1-212-555-6987, most of us omit the "1" when giving someone our number. When communicating with someone who has a different country code, they will understand that, and will know to add the "1" on the front. Again, it is an easy way to show respect – add the "1".

> Take a look at a business card from someone outside of the US – their country code is listed at the beginning of all of their phone numbers. Now look at yours (assuming you are based in the US) – there is a pretty good chance it does not. I'm not saying this is the end of the world, but it is a little myopic.

The world is round (not everyone is in your timezone)

When you are meeting with people in other time zones, consider their schedule as well as yours. If you are on a late night call from New York and meeting with people in Hong Kong, greet them with "good morning". It's simple and might sound trivial, but it shows respect.

Logistics: Eating and drinking

When you are out of the office with co-workers or clients you should approach everything you do as if you were in the office or at a client location.

Lunch

In my opinion, on most days lunch is part of your job. Take the opportunity to eat with your co-workers and build relationships with them. If you are on a client site, you will often have the opportunity to eat with client personnel. Do this. If one of your superiors is not there, pay for it (check with your Senior/Manager first, but they will almost always encourage you to do this. Ask for guidelines as to how much you can spend.). This may be the only opportunity you get to spend time with your client in a less-formal setting, and it almost always results in a better relationship with them.

Never forget that lunch, like other eating and drinking events discussed here, is part of your job, so you should exercise the same level of professionalism expected of you in the office, whether you are just with other staff or with a client CEO.

Holiday parties/company outings

Many people approach holiday parties and company outings as another opportunity to eat and drink. And drink, and drink. If you walked into the last hour of any of these events, at least 75% of the people there will be either drunk or very drunk, and it is entirely possible that one or more of them has made a complete fool of themselves. This is not college – there are no awards for displaying your amazing capacity for consuming alcohol. Think about it – there are only three possible outcomes from these events:

1. You are not noticed or remembered – You either didn't show up, or you did show up and spoke to a small group of friends and colleagues with whom you already have relationships. This is a perfectly acceptable option, but you are missing a chance to network and at least get introduced to a few of the higher-ups.
2. You are noticed, but not remembered – You showed up, nursed a drink or two (and by the way, non-alcoholic is a fine choice here) and got yourself introduced to a few new people. This is a perfect networking event and it's a good idea to take advantage of it.
3. You are noticed AND remembered – Let's face it, the people that get remembered from holiday parties and company outings are ALMOST ALWAYS the ones who are going to be remembered for all of the wrong reasons. This is a really easy and stupid way to damage your career.

You will notice that there is very little upside, and a HUGE potential downside at these events. Your goal is to be noticed and then forgotten.

If you are going to drink, drink with your friends some other time and place, NOT with your whole office. And don't worry, the Partners that want to hang out and drink with a bunch of young people (and there are more than a few) WILL FIND YOU.

Out-of-office events

I know it might not feel like a work event, but if you are out with people from work, you need to treat it like work. You can do harm to your career at these events, and inappropriate actions (based on the standards and expectations that exist IN THE OFFICE) at these events can get you fired.

Basic skills: Time management

A consumer products company makes money by taking raw materials and producing something they can sell to consumers. A professional services firm makes money by taking you, or more specifically your time, and producing something they can sell to clients. You are your firm's raw materials, and the more productive you are with your time, the more valuable you are to your firm.

Managing priorities

One of the more challenging aspects of your career in a large professional services firm is the fact that you will have multiple "bosses". As a Staff, you will likely be involved in multiple concurrent projects, each of which is headed by a Senior or Manager who will be directing your efforts. You may also have one or more Directors or Partners who have you working on client-chargeable work or internal projects. You will constantly be faced with deadlines and priorities that will not work so nicely together.

Chapter 3: Managing your work

When you receive multiple priorities from different individuals, you can easily fall into the trap of trying to meet every deadline, putting you into a situation where you cannot meet them all. You must avoid this whenever possible, and it's actually not that hard to manage; **do not attempt to manage these priorities by yourself.** You need to communicate your priorities, as you understand them, to the individuals who are asking you to perform work for them, and let them determine what your overall priorities should be.

For instance, let's say you are working on an audit report that has a deadline of this Friday, and a Partner calls you into their office to discuss a proposal on which they would like your help – they need you to modify a presentation that you helped develop for a previous pursuit. When they tell you that they need the presentation done by Thursday, don't simply tell them "sure," and walk back to your desk to start working on it. Instead, tell them you would like to help, but you have other tasks that you need to complete. Explain your other current responsibilities and deadlines, and ask them to help you set your priorities. If, during your discussion, they don't reach out to the Senior or Manager in charge of the project for which you are completing the audit report due Friday, YOU need to contact the Senior or Manager immediately after your meeting with the Partner and make sure they are aware of your additional responsibilities.

While it is not your job to set priorities on concurrent items on your to-do list, it IS your responsibility to ensure that all of your various "bosses" are aware of, and in agreement with, the priorities that have been set for you. Failing to properly managing priorities usually leads to multiple deadlines missed and just as many bosses upset.

Budgets

There is a budget for virtually everything you do. In college, you had the luxury of, if you thought something you were producing was not to your satisfaction, spending as much time on it as you liked. That is not the case now. If you have two hours to complete a task, you are expected to complete it in two hours or less. The instant you know that you are going to exceed a budget, you must contact the person to whom you are reporting and consult with them.

This doesn't mean you have no leeway whatsoever – if you have multiple tasks to complete, with a total budget of eight hours, and you will be able to complete all of them in that eight-hour period, you don't need to run to your Senior every time a single task goes over by 15 minutes.

Remember, your time gets charged to the job, and ultimately the client must either pay for the time, or the firm must write it off. Causing the firm to unexpectedly write off your time is a great way to get fired.

Basic skills: Meetings

You are going to spend a fair amount of time in meetings. Most people, understandably, don't like meetings because they can be inefficient and ineffective. Too many meetings lack strong leadership, and don't fully accomplish their purpose, and in many cases the purpose is not well-defined.

Meetings are obviously necessary at some level, and they can be efficient and productive (and a LOT more enjoyable) if you follow a few basic rules in preparing for and running them.

Meeting preparation

With very few exceptions, you should never walk into a meeting cold. For any meeting you attend, you should spend at least a few minutes (possibly much more depending on the meeting) preparing for the meeting. If you are meeting with a client on an engagement, review the topics that will be covered either by looking at related client documentation or other resources (Google them – you might discover something critical that has impacted them in the recent past). Not only will it clear your mind of all of the other things that are going on and help you focus when you are in the meeting, but it shows a tremendous amount of respect for the other meeting participants.

> I had a first-year Staff a few years ago who struggled in her first few months and was not viewed as an "A" player in our practice. She was part of the team that met a client to plan work in a niche part of their business where we had relatively little experience. During the meeting, she did not speak a lot (although she took pretty good notes, as I recall). However, at one point during the meeting, as the client was describing their segment's business model she asked an amazingly insightful question that could only have been asked by someone who knew their business relatively well. After the meeting I asked her how she knew to ask that question. She had spent about an hour preparing for a 30-minute meeting, and had done some very detailed follow-up on a single item she found in their annual report that she thought might be related to this small business segment. That single event allowed her to build trust with that client individual very quickly, and less than a year later she was the in-charge on additional work we performed for that group.

Running meetings

As a staff person, you will get the opportunity to run meetings. Some of these will be small meetings with client personnel where you are trying to get specific information like an understanding of a particular process. Others will be internal meetings to convey information or solve specific problems. If you are in charge of running the meeting it is crucial that you do the following in preparation:

1. Determine the purpose of the meeting. You should take the time to understand and document what you, collectively, need to have as the outcome of the meeting. If it is not completely straight-forward, you should reach out to the other meeting participants to get their input.

2. Document an agenda. You don't necessarily need to get into specific timing for specific topics, but you do need a list of items to be covered, and again, you do not need to figure this all out yourself, but it is YOUR responsibility to make sure this information is ready in advance of the meeting. It is usually appropriate to distribute the agenda ahead of time so others can be prepared as well.

3. Spend enough time preparing for the meeting to identify all of the information you need, including other documents that may support the discussion.

Once the meeting starts, the person running the meeting (you, in this case) should:

1. If some or all of the parties are attending via a conference call, conduct a quick roll call so that everyone knows who all of the meeting participants are.

2. Ask if anyone has a hard stop when the meeting is scheduled to end. This will help tremendously should the meeting start to run over, and it shows respect for the other parties.

3. Articulate the purpose of the meeting. Make sure everyone is in agreement as to what the desired outcome/output will be.

4. Quickly run through the agenda to see if anyone has any questions. You may need to make adjustments on the fly if a topic needs to be added to the agenda.

5. Keep the meeting moving. Just because the meeting is scheduled for an hour, it doesn't mean you should take the full time if you can move through the necessary topics in less time.

6. Keep meticulous notes. If there is another Staff in the meeting, you can ask them (ahead of time) to take notes, but if you are the only staff there, you should assume that this is your responsibility.

7. At the end of the meeting, go over any tasks that have been assigned (additional documents or information needed, next steps, etc.) and ensure that the responsible parties (including you!) are clear as to what is expected and when it is expected.

Taking notes

When you are invited to a meeting with a client or prospective client (this also applies to certain internal meetings, like engagement planning), there is a pretty good chance you are the lowest-ranking person in the group. While you are probably encouraged to participate if you have something of value to add, you should expect that part of your job is to take notes. You can actually use this role to your advantage – if you are taking good, detailed notes, you will have opportunities to ask clarification questions. This is a great way for you to contribute to the meeting, as it does not require a great deal of experience (which you do not have), and shows the whole team that you are taking your job seriously.

When the meeting is over, organize your notes and distribute them to the INTERNAL meeting participants. This happens too rarely, and will make a very favorable impression on your superiors.

Basic skills: Writing

You are going to spend a LOT of time writing. Get good at it, and quickly, because most of the value you add to your firm and to your clients is either in the form of written documents or will be supported by written documents. In many ways, your value to the organization, and therefore your ability to get promoted, will be a direct result of how quickly you can learn to write effectively enough to minimize the amount of review that your superiors have to perform on your written work.

Effective writing

You have probably been writing for years. Most of you are going to need to re-learn how to write, because the type of writing most of us did in high school and college is not effective in a business environment.

1. As much as possible, use plain English. Try to avoid big words when small ones will do. Do not try to sound official when you do not absolutely need to. Remember, the primary purpose of your document is to communicate, not to try to sound as smart as you can.

2. You are not getting paid by the word. Shorter is better. See?

3. Know who your audience is, and write accordingly. Read each section or paragraph after you write it FROM THE POINT OF VIEW OF THE ULTIMATE AUDIENCE, to determine if a) they will understand it and b) it delivers the intended message.

4. Always keep in the front of your mind WHO the audience is for whatever you are writing. You are writing for the reader, not for yourself.

5. I am repeating myself, but this is important. Do not just write something and then pass it up for review. Write, then read, then edit, then read again, and repeat as necessary. Always deliver a document that YOU think is ready for the client without further review.

I have two specific pet peeves regarding writing:

Write a sentence containing the word "currently." Now take that word out. Your sentence is now shorter and you have not changed the meaning AT ALL.

The words "utilize" and "use" mean virtually the same thing. One sounds pretentious and the other is shorter. Simple choice.

Reports and presentations

You will spend a lot of time over the course of your career writing reports or preparing presentations for yourself and others. You need to get into the habit of creating finished products. When someone (say, a client) receives a report with basic errors in it (even "stupid" things like formatting inconsistency), it causes them to have a much lower level of confidence in the message (and in the person sending it!), even when the message is spot on.

Creating finished products means:

1. Pay attention to spelling and grammar and get it right
2. Use consistent fonts and font sizes
3. When you think you are finished, check how the final document will look by running print preview, and make sure the alignment, page breaks, and other formatting is optimized
4. When you REALLY think you are finished, take a short break and then re-read every single word – you will always find something to correct or something you could write more clearly.

Do NOT rely on spell-check to catch everything. A few years ago one of my colleagues sent out a draft report for a client going through an Initial Public Offering. The report was returned with the following comment: "On page 22, please change the date from May 23 to May 25, and on page 56, please change the word Pubic to Public."

Managing your work

This may seem tedious, but believe me, it is important. Way too often, I have reviewed reports or presentations prepared by others that are rife with spelling, grammatical and formatting errors. The job of a reviewer is usually to focus on content and messaging; having to fix things that my Staff or Senior (or in some cases even MANAGER) should have taken care of is very frustrating.

Basic skills: Documentation

Documentation is a fundamental skill, and one that you should focus a lot of time on early in your career. You need to develop good habits so that as you get promoted and your workload increases, you automatically consider the appropriate documentation methods for each given situation. In addition, when you are given the responsibility for managing others, you will be expected to teach them sound documentation principles. Your firm will spend a lot of time and money teaching you to document well (much of this learning will be on-the-job), and I will not attempt to teach you this. There are a few fundamentals that have helped me over the years:

1. You are documenting for the benefit of the reviewer, not for your own benefit. Make sure that your documentation makes sense to others, not just to you.
2. Your documentation needs to stand on its own. It needs to make sense without you having to sit next to the reviewer and explain it to them.
3. Documentation applies to all aspects of a project, from planning, during execution of that plan (or work program) and all the way through reporting.
4. Pay particular attention to documenting not just what you do, but the logic behind it. If you draw a conclusion about something, make sure you document your logic behind reaching that conclusion.

5. Do not provide more documentation than is needed. All documentation is discoverable, so if you attach a 600-page word file, and all you have reviewed is the table of contents and one section, that is all you should include. If you include that 600-page file, you are responsible for reading EVERY SINGLE WORD in that document.

6. If you didn't document it, you didn't do it. I repeat this one a LOT.

> When you were in school, particularly in math classes, you were often told that you could not simply provide the answer – you were also required to "show your work." You should think of documentation the same way.

Basic skills: Speaking and listening

You are in a people business. Your skill in verbal communication will likely be important.

Speaking up

Attention! All extroverts: You are relatively inexperienced and you probably need to take that into consideration when you have the opportunity to express your opinion. Make sure your input is respectful and fully considers the fact that some of the people you are working with have been in the work force longer than you have been alive. Don't ask stupid questions in front of a client – save them for your Senior or Manager.

Attention! All introverts: You were hired because the firm believes you have something to offer. If all you do is keep your head down and produce excellent work products, you run the real risk that your contribution is not fully recognized. You need to get comfortable, and quickly, with speaking your mind (tactfully, of course).

Chapter 3: Managing your work

Listening

You will learn a lot more by listening than by talking. Listen. Take notes. When you are not clear about something, ask questions. As a Staff, you were not hired because of what you know, but because of what you can learn and apply.

Development as a professional: Developing your network

It's never too early to start building your network. From this point forward, most of you will just get busier and busier until you retire. You might as well start forming strong network-building habits now. Network building is a skill, and something you will get better at the more you work at it. If you put it off for a year, you will be one year behind for the rest of your life.

Client relationships

Your clients pay your salary. Without clients, your firm is nothing, and you don't have a job. They deserve, and have a right to expect, your attention and respect. So get to know them – it is not just the job of your Senior Managers and Partners to foster relationships with client personnel. While you, as a Staff, probably don't have access to, or the slightest basis for a relationship with, your client's CEO, the client personnel you DO interact with on a daily basis are likely people with whom you can develop relationships. There are several positive outcomes from this:

1. It will make your job easier – you will almost definitely need the cooperation of client personnel to complete your work in an efficient manner, and it's virtually impossible to develop trust without personal connection.

2. It will help you grow professionally – understanding the work that you are doing from your client's point of view will help you better understand WHY you are doing what you are doing.

3. The client personnel with whom you regularly interact are your best source for identifying other opportunities for your firm at that client.

4. It makes your job more enjoyable – you spend a lot of time with these people, so connecting on a personal level usually makes what you are doing feel less like a "job."

5. The Manager of Accounts Payable you befriend today will be the CFO when you are a Partner.

Understand that, especially with lower-level personnel, your client may view you with apprehension and even suspicion. You are an outsider who is examining, in detail, what they do on a day-to-day basis, and you are often being paid to find stuff they are doing wrong.

Professional associations

You may have belonged to Beta Alpha Psi or another similar organization while you were in school. There is no reason you can't stay involved now that you are in the professional world. However, now that you ARE in the professional world, there is an amazingly wide variety of professional groups you can also join. Pick one or two of these (ask your advisor or other superiors for ideas) and try it out. It's not like you are making a life-long commitment, and the opportunities to interact with others in the industry are invaluable. You might even enjoy it.

Development as a professional: Improving your performance

Don't just put your head down and work. You are your most important "client" and if you don't take advantage of the opportunity to constantly improve your performance, you will not be successful, and probably won't like your job very much.

Chapter 3: Managing your work

Receiving feedback

You will be constantly evaluated - during projects, at the end of projects and periodically throughout the year. This is true at EVERY level of the firm, and most people get comfortable with that fact, at least somewhat, pretty early in their career. You need to accept this and not take it personally. The person providing this feedback has a vested interest in your success, so accept it for what it is – an opportunity for you to improve yourself and your performance. It may be hard (in fact, it WILL be), but you cannot allow yourself to get defensive; DO NOT ARGUE. Think about it this way, even if you are doing something perfectly, the fact that someone (or someones) thinks that you need to improve some aspect of what you are doing is, in and of itself, an issue for you. Do not even attempt to convince them that they are wrong because you will fail, and run the real risk of being tagged (correctly, by the way) as someone who cannot take feedback. There ARE a few things you can do to make this a very positive experience for both of you:

1. Make sure you fully understand the feedback you are receiving – ask questions
2. Ask for examples
3. Ask the reviewer to help you identify ways you can improve on the areas you are discussing
4. Periodically meet with the person providing the feedback to check on their impression of your progress

That last point is where most people fail. It is much easier to just do your best and not run the risk of being told that the improvement you think you are making is not actually improvement or is not being recognized. However, the very act of following up on these issues will help you improve your performance, and is the easiest way to ensure that people understand your sincere desire to develop yourself.

Chapter 3: Managing your work

You will receive feedback (review notes) on virtually everything you produce. Every workpaper, report, memo, presentation and anything else you create will come back to you with a LOT of changes, comments and questions. Again, DO NOT TAKE THIS PERSONALLY. I have seen countless documents, prepared by PARTNERS, come back to them in a sea of red ink after another Partner has reviewed them.

Think

You are likely intelligent (if not, put this book down and start looking for another job now), and you were hired to use your brain. Do not, even with the simplest of tasks, just mindlessly execute what you have been asked to do. You should always keep the following in mind:

1. Why am I doing this?
2. Is this going as anticipated by me and by the person who assigned it to me? (and if not, should I consult them before I go further?)
3. Is there a way to do this better or faster?
4. What is the budget for this task, and am I going to meet it (and if not, have I communicated this to my superior)?

Understand why

You will be expected to be able to answer detailed questions about your work. Make sure you understand each task you are given – every step you are expected to complete in a given work program – and make sure you understand WHY each step is being performed. Understanding why will put you in a much better position to make adjustments (or at least suggest adjustments) when things don't go exactly as anticipated.

Chapter 3: Managing your work

Human beings are never finished products. Close your eyes (first read this paragraph, THEN close your eyes), picture yourself when you entered college, and consider how much you have grown, intellectually and emotionally, since then. Then open your eyes and read the next paragraph.

You will likely grow more in the next year than you did over that four- or five-year period. I remember thinking, after my first month of work as a professional, "I learned more in the last month than I did during four years (ok, four and a half years) of college."

Pay attention to your personal growth, it will make you a better employee and a better person.

Work/Life balance

One could write an entire book on this subject, and several people have. I will just say this:

For the majority of you, especially at this stage of your career, your job is the most important thing you do on a day-to-day basis. I am NOT saying it is more important than taking care of a sick parent or taking care of your children, but it IS immeasurably more important than playing in a softball league, hanging out with friends, and the like. You should set your priorities accordingly. If you are not willing to make your job a top priority, you are not a bad person – however you should probably find another job.

> Many individuals have a work persona that is very different from their "real" self, outside of work. This, in my opinion, is waaaaaay too stressful. To me, work/life balance early in your career is about merging those two selves - I believe it makes you a more effective employee, and makes it much easier to enjoy your work.

Chapter 3: Managing your work

Spend time reflecting

No matter how busy you are, try to set aside some time each day to reflect on your job. You will be happier, and a much better employee. This can be as simple as spending 15 minutes at the end of each day asking yourself what you learned that day, what relationships you developed, or what your priorities should be tomorrow.

Have fun

You will be spending way too much time working to be miserable, or even indifferent in your day-to-day work. I have found the vast majority of people in this career to be very passionate about what they do, and that is a great thing. Try to not forget that YOU CHOSE THIS JOB, and likely for good reason. Besides, people will naturally gravitate towards people who enjoy what they do.

Even when performing seemingly mundane tasks, I have found it to be worthwhile to remind myself what I am getting out of that task. Sometimes the only benefit to me is learning how to be a professional and get done what needs to get done - even this is a highly valuable lesson. I am developing my relationship with whoever gave me the task by getting it done well and on time – this is actually priceless.

Remember, no matter what you are doing, you probably have an opportunity to enhance or damage the trust someone else has in you.

Chapter 3: Managing your work

Control your emotions

You are a grown up, so act like one. People will make you mad or frustrated, but if you react "instinctively" to the stimuli that cause you to feel this way, you are, in essence, giving someone else control over your actions. I'm not saying that I never get mad, but if I display anger, it is almost always:

- on purpose,
- after a fair amount of thought, and
- the method I have determined most likely to get the response that I want.

Chapter 4: Exceeding expectations

"Exceeding expectations" is a phrase that gets thrown around a LOT in your firm. We have to exceed our clients' expectations. You are asked to exceed expectations on individual projects. Most importantly (to you), your overall performance is supposed to "exceed expectations" in order for you to be highly rated (and promoted). Awesome. What the heck does this actually mean?

Certainly, part of this is related to operating at a level above your current level (a Staff person operating as a Senior). You should obviously strive to do this, but by itself, this approach is not sustainable. Think about it; if you ARE able to operate as a Senior while you are at the Staff level, the instant you get promoted you will no longer be exceeding expectations.

There are several things that you can do that give you a fighting chance of being one of those people (and there are not a lot) who seem to exist in a permanent state of "exceeding expectations."

Ownership

I have this listed first for a reason. The single quality I have seen with every high performer, and that is absent in every poor performer, is the ability and willingness to take ownership for the projects and clients they serve. If you only remember one thing from this book, make it this section.

Ownership does NOT mean you are in charge. It is not a power thing – it is a responsibility thing.

Ownership starts with demonstrating the ability and consistent willingness to take full responsibility for tasks that are assigned to you. To fully demonstrate this quality, however, you need to assume, at a very personal level, responsibility for doing all that you can (at the direction of your superiors) to assist in completing the tasks assigned to your entire project team(s). This means constantly seeking to understand ALL of the tasks involved in an engagement, and looking for ways to help your fellow staff and your Seniors and Managers wherever you can. It means realizing that your team will get recognized for what you, collectively, accomplish. It means NOT simply getting "your" work done and then leaving at 5:00 when others on your team are still working on "their" tasks. You are not finished until the team is finished.

An ownership object lesson:

Let's say you have a report that you are updating for your Manager. It needs to be completed by Friday; it's Monday afternoon and you have made your latest changes. The report is ready for your Manager to review, and you email it to her – Yay! You are finished early!

Correction! You are NOT finished. If you understand the concept of ownership, you are fully aware that you are not finished until the report is ready for your client, and that cannot happen until your Manager has reviewed the report and you have made any changes identified during that review. In addition, in all likelihood, the Partner will need to review the report, and even more changes will be necessitated by that review.

So, what should you do on that Monday afternoon after you have emailed the report to your Manager? Contact the Manager and tell her that the report is in her in-box, ready for her review. When you find out that she is headed for the airport in a couple of hours to fly to a client location, print off a copy of the report and give it to her so that if she has time, she can easily review the report on the plane. Schedule a follow-up meeting with her on Tuesday to go over her comments, and schedule time immediately after that meeting for you to make any necessary changes to the report.

Chapter 4: Exceeding expectations

Managing your career

Perhaps the most consistent mistake I have seen from solid performers is that they simply do their job, expecting that their performance alone will catapult them up the ranks in their firm. Your firm may provide you with a counselor, and others may take an interest in helping you maximize your potential, but there is no substitute for YOU, managing your own career. You should spend time thinking about your career progression, honestly assessing your own performance, capitalizing on your strengths and making professional improvements where you need them. You must be PROACTIVE in undertaking this, not reactive. Don't coast – it's a habit that, once formed, is almost impossible to break.

Most firms have an annual promotion cycle. Too many individuals enter this process with hopes of being promoted, not having a solid understanding of what they needed to do in the last year to warrant that consideration.

If you expect to get promoted, the process starts at the beginning of the year. You need to have a frank discussion with your counselor to understand if your promotion is possible, and if so, discuss the things you will need to accomplish or improve upon to get promoted. You need to meet regularly with your counselor to track your progress, and you need to demonstrate clearly that you are progressing adequately. If you do those things, you can have a reasonable expectation that you will be considered for promotion during the next promotion cycle.

If you do not spend the time to understand what you need to accomplish in order to be considered promotion-worthy, or do not ensure that you adequately demonstrate those accomplishments throughout the year, you will likely not get promoted.

Promotions don't just happen; you have to make them happen.

Chapter 4: Exceeding expectations

Mentors

I just told you that it is up to YOU to drive your career forward. That does not mean that you will be able to achieve what you want to without help. Seek out someone who:

1. Works in your group, preferably on one or more of your jobs
2. Is the kind of person and performer you would like to emulate
3. Is recognized as a high performer
4. Is interested in developing a professional relationship with you

Pay close attention to these criteria, as you may well be tying your career progression, at least in part, to this individual. The higher they progress in the firm, the more help they can be to you.

The people who make the best mentors fully understand the need for, and genuinely enjoy, finding and developing talent (in this case, you). They will almost certainly initiate (informally) relationships with those individuals they see as worthy mentees. Pay attention; when you find yourself on the cusp of one of these relationships, TAKE ADVANTAGE OF IT. Any meaningful relationship requires the willing participation of both parties, and if they have already taken the first steps, you need to take the next steps.

Perhaps the most important aspect of having a mentor is that someone besides you is interested in your career development, and that individual likely has the ability and influence to really help you further your career.

Chapter 4: Exceeding expectations

Seeking feedback

Your firm has several mechanisms in place designed to provide you with feedback on your performance. While some (very few, unfortunately) people are very diligent about providing formal feedback every time they are supposed to, it is not unusual for many people to go for months at a time without receiving real feedback.

Make it a point to regularly seek out feedback from the people directly above you on projects, and from other Seniors and Managers for whom you work. Most of them will not object to you setting up regular (monthly is a good target) meetings to discuss how you are doing, and to follow up on items they have brought to your attention in previous feedback sessions. It is not enough, however, to just get the meetings on their calendars; many of them will be insanely busy, and you will need to be persistent in making the meetings happen on a regular basis.

A good number of your peers will set these meetings up with the best of intentions. Most will not follow up and will suffer as a result.

Recently, I worked for a Partner with whom I had developed a very strong mentor/mentee relationship. He not only headed up my practice, but had taken a keen interest in my career. The only problem was, as is the case with many successful people, his schedule made it very difficult to carve out time to meet on a regular basis.

My solution? I knew that when he was in the office, he usually left right at 6:00 to catch his train home. I got in the habit of walking to his train station with him (after which, I walked back to the office – my train left from a different station), which gave me 10-15 minutes of relatively undivided attention a couple of times per week.

Chapter 4: Exceeding expectations

Building relationships

It's a small world, and the relationships you build will not only help you right now, but 10, 20 and even 30 years down the road. Build relationships with your professional superiors and peers, and also with executive assistants, tech support personnel, HR personnel and anyone else you interact with on any regular basis. I'm not telling you to go out to lunch or for drinks with all of them, but remember their names and get to know them a little bit. I promise you, being on a first-name basis with the executive assistant for one of your client executives or with one of your office tech support specialists will help you immensely at some point.

Besides, you are in a people business. Be that person who seems to know EVERYBODY.

Building a team

One of the most important, in fact, maybe **the** most important skill you will need to develop throughout your career is learning how to recognize and develop talent. You develop first one team, and then multiple teams underneath you of people who you can depend on to deliver quality work for you. This happens one person at a time, and you cannot start this process too early. You need people underneath you who are willing and able to not only get their work done, but to gradually take on the bulk of your responsibilities. **You cannot reasonably take on the responsibilities of the person above you (and get promoted) unless you first have people underneath you to take on your work** – there just aren't enough hours in the day for you to do both.

Chapter 4: Exceeding expectations

Climbing

Your relationships with your direct peers will have a large impact on your ability to achieve long-term success and get regularly promoted in your firm. You should focus on building and strengthening these bonds as early as possible. While quite a few ambitious individuals (at all levels) focus virtually all of their attention on their superiors (i.e., kissing up), this will eventually catch up to most of them, as they will have a difficult time building teams and being trusted by their peers.

You are in a career where success is largely measured by promotion. While you are part of a team, you are also in constant competition with your peers. This can be very healthy if you are willing to embrace the concept that success at your firm is not a zero-sum game. Your success does not need to come at the expense of your peers, and vise-versa. In fact, your success can and should benefit your peers.

It is a simple fact that at some point, one or more of your peer group will get promoted ahead of the rest. When this happens, whether you are promoted ahead of some of your peers or some of your peers get promoted ahead of you, you will have an opportunity to strengthen your position with the firm...if you have laid the appropriate groundwork and built strong relationships with your peer group.

If you get promoted ahead of your peers: Your former peers are primary candidates to work directly for you. If you have developed strong relationships with them, you have a huge head-start in developing your "team" as described in the section above.

If your peer gets promoted ahead of you: This person is now in a good position to help you move up. If you have developed a strong relationship with him/her, they may be able to help you get on projects that you find desirable, and can help position you better for future promotion cycles.

Chapter 4: Exceeding expectations

At 5:00

Your office may close at 5:00, but as I pointed out previously, you have entered a career that often requires close to a 24/7 commitment. If you don't have tasks that require you to work late, you should, on a regular basis, stop by your Senior's or Manager's desk as your office is "closing" for the day, and find out if there is anything you can help them with. You will get a lot more responsibility, it will accelerate your career development, and will usually result in your involvement in some pretty cool stuff (research, proposals and the like).

> Several years ago I was working on a deliverable for a client late into the evening. I expected I would be up all night completing it. At about 9:00pm, one of my Seniors called me on his way home from work to see how my day went. I told him what I was working on and told him to have a good night.
>
> About 30 minutes later, he showed up in the office to help me. We completed the work at about 2:00am. I cited this example in the promotion meetings a few months later, and it was one of the factors that lead to his promotion to Manager that year.

What to do when you make a mistake

Mistakes happen every day, at every level in your firm. While you should certainly strive to minimize the number of mistakes you make, it is not a realistic goal to eliminate all mistakes. After all, if you are successful, you will constantly be given new and larger responsibilities, and learning to manage those responsibilities will almost never be a seamless process. Instead, you should strive to be one of those people that takes advantage of their mistakes by accepting them and learning from them.

Chapter 4: Exceeding expectations

If you make a mistake and you realize it before it is pointed out to you: Obviously, fix it if you can. If it in any way impacts others on your team or, more importantly, a client, IMMEDIATELY bring it to the attention of your superiors. Everyone makes mistakes, and there are almost no mistakes from which you cannot recover. Except for trying to hide a mistake.

If you make a mistake and it is brought to your attention by a peer: Treat this the same way as a mistake you discovered yourself.

If you make a mistake and it is brought to your attention by one of your superiors: DO NOT GET DEFENSIVE. Listen – you probably have an opportunity to learn something. It is very easy to get the reputation of not being able to take constructive criticism, and if you consistently make the mistake of trying to argue your way out of problems that are brought to your attention, people will simply stop staffing you on their jobs. Your career, at least with your current firm, will be very short.

If you make a mistake and it is brought to your attention by a client: Believe it or not, this can actually have a very positive outcome – if you handle it correctly. Again, everyone makes mistakes; not everyone handles them well. How you deal with a mistake will have a much more lasting impression than the mistake itself. If your client sees that you know how to deal with your mistakes properly, they are more likely to respect you, and place trust in you going forward. When this happens (and it will):

1. Do not argue (think about it this way – if your client thinks there is a problem, that, in and of itself, is a problem)
2. Do not EVER place the blame on someone else (even if it is their fault)
3. Read steps 1 and 2 again

Chapter 4: Exceeding expectations

4. Tell the client you will work with your team to rectify the problem. Do not commit to any specific remediation of the problem – those commitments are above your pay grade.
5. Immediately inform your supervisors – they will work with the client to determine the appropriate action.
6. Figure out what you and your team need to do to make sure the problem does not happen again.

When you are presented with a mistake, all of your focus should be on how to fix it. You can worry later about why it happened (see step 6 above – there is a reason that it is preceded by five other steps). I have seen a great many upset clients become once-again-happy clients because the response they got from their service provider was immediately "what do we need to do to fix this?" and then the service provider delivered the requested resolution.

Chapter 5: Rules

Over the years, I have developed a list of basic rules that I still turn to on a regular basis. While these do not necessarily represent brilliant insight, it is amazing how often I need to remind myself of them (and they are MY rules!). While this represents my personal view of the professional world, I believe these are universal. And I am astonished at how many people regularly violate one or more of them.

Rule 1: Show up

"Eighty percent of success is showing up" per Woody Allen, and a lot of others. I'm not sure about the percentage, but it's number one on my list for a reason. All of the other things you need to do to be successful start with this.

Difficult meeting? Feeling tired? Want to avoid a difficult situation? It's always easier in the short term to avoid or put off something, but it's ALWAYS better to deal with things head-on. Show up, and you always have a chance to create the best solution for your firm, your team and yourself.

> I have encountered several people over the course of my career who, when they have a difficult situation (or maybe just uncomfortable for them), seem to get sick, or have something else come up. I know people get sick, and things DO come up, but for some people, it happens a lot more often than it should. They will rationalize their (probably) subconscious decision (yes, I said "decision") to miss that thing they want so badly to avoid, and will even lie to themselves about it.
>
> Trust me on two things: (1) It's noticed and will negatively impact your career and (2) much more often than not, things turn out better than a fearful imagination had them turning out.

Rules

Chapter 5: Rules

Rule 2:   Be there

No matter what situation you are in, you will achieve more success by focusing on what you are doing NOW. If you are in a meeting, focus on that meeting. If you are reviewing a document, focus on that document. Whatever you are doing, commit completely to it, and you will not only do it better, you will get more personal development and satisfaction out of it. Seriously, very few things annoy me more than people sending texts or ON THEIR COMPUTER during a meeting. If something is that important, leave the meeting and deal with it or don't come to the meeting in the first place.

Rule 3:   Be on time

For a significant portion of my life I was perpetually late. To everything. Among other causes, what I later realized is that I would have an understanding of how long it took to get somewhere ASSUMING THERE WERE NO DELAYS WHATSOEVER, and that is the amount of time I would give myself to get there. At one point in my life, one of my friends pulled me aside and explained the following:

> When you are late for something, you are, basically, telling the person or people who are waiting for you "my time is more important than yours." It's selfish.

"Be on time" actually means "be a little bit early". It is annoying when people walk into a 9:00am meeting right at 9:00. While they spend time greeting the other attendees and getting settled into their chair, they are delaying the start of the meeting. Get in the habit of showing up five minutes early.

Rule 4: Initiate communication on the left side of the communication hierarchy

Technology constantly gives us additional communication methods. While these can create efficiency, there is an increased burden on the communicator to select the appropriate method. There are two basic factors to consider:

1. Body language and voice inflection – given that research shows that approximately 90% of communication is based on something other than the actual words that are spoken, body language and voice inflection are incredibly important.
2. Synchronous vs. asynchronous communication – with some notable exceptions (e.g., sharing large amounts of data, creating a documentation trail) synchronous communication is VASTLY more efficient than asynchronous communication (we have all experienced long email conversations, covering multiple days, that could have been averted by a single, five-minute phone call).

In general, you should favor a communication method on the left side of the following hierarchy:

in person > video conference > phone call > text > email > silence

> There are many situations where email is the necessary communication method. Keep in mind that many people receive hundreds of emails in a given day, and might not be able to get through all of their email for days at a time. If you send someone an email that you need them to review sooner rather than later, you should contact that person either in person, on the phone or by text (making sure they respond!), letting them know what you have just sent.

Rules

Chapter 5: Rules

Rule 5: Own your tasks

When you are given a task or responsibility, the person assigning it to you likely expects you to own it all the way through completion. That means it is your responsibility to (a) get it done, and (b) regularly communicate your progress back to the person who assigned the task to you.

Get it done: This means just that – the task is yours to complete. You have primary responsibility to overcome whatever speed bumps you encounter on that path. It is not acceptable, when asked about your progress, to reply "I needed additional information from Andy. I sent him an email last week and he hasn't gotten back to me yet." First of all, let's hope you followed Rule 4 when you sent the email. If Andy doesn't reply to the email in a timely manner, go to his desk, call him, text him, whatever it takes. If you have no luck with these, discuss it with the person who assigned the task to you.

Regularly communicate your progress back to the person who assigned the task to you: Don't make them ask you about your progress; it will significantly hinder your ability to establish yourself as trustworthy. Reach out to them on a regular basis to let them know your progress (when you are initially assigned the task, ask them how often they would like you to report your progress). When you have completed the task, don't just send an email letting them know you are finished – they might not see it right away. See Rule 4.

> Every time someone gives you something to do, make sure you understand when it is needed and the relative importance of the task – do NOT assume that you can figure that out by yourself, even if you have completed similar tasks in the past.

Chapter 5: Rules

Rule 6:   Consider the implications of personal communication
           vs. group communication

There is a huge difference between what you say one-on-one and what you say to two or more people. When you discuss anything with a single person, in private, there is a level of confidentiality that you should be able to assume. The minute you discuss something in a group of three (including yourself) or more, even if you have discussed the exact same thing with each of the other people in a one-on-one setting, you lose that level of confidentiality.

For example, even if you say something while you are with two other people and *explicitly tell them* that they should not repeat it to anyone, they will subconsciously treat that information more loosely than if you had told them one-on-one. It might just be that they feel more comfortable discussing the same topic between the two of them, and someone else overhears them. They are much more likely to talk about it with someone else they both trust. They are more likely to bring it up when you are with one of them and someone else they think is in your circle of trust. This can create huge problems for you that could have been avoided if you kept this rule in mind.

There is always, of course, the risk that something you tell one person in confidence is divulged by that person to another. However, that risk is much lower if you have never discussed it with more than one person at a time.

There are times when it is perfectly appropriate or even necessary to discuss sensitive or confidential information with more than one person at a time, but my point is this: Think before you do.

Chapter 5: Rules

Rule 7: **If you are not going to add anything of value, STOP TALKING**

Internal meetings often take a lot longer than they need to because attention-starved, self-important knuckleheads not only feel the need to let everyone else know that they agree with a decision or conclusion, but somehow feel the need to also explain (sometimes in great detail) WHY they agree with everyone else. This seems silly, but pay attention in a few meetings, and you will find yourself smiling to yourself at the same time you start to calculate the amount of time wasted by this activity. If the person moderating the meeting asks you if you have anything to add, and you do not, it is perfectly acceptable to say "I agree" or "I have nothing to add." If they want more color, they will ask you for it.

This can also apply in one-on-one situations. I have numerous (literally dozens right off the top of my head) examples I could cite here, but I will do you the favor of giving you just one.

I had a Senior approach me about a training class she wanted to attend. The topic was perfect for an upcoming assignment, and she wanted to be as prepared as possible. I thought it was a no-brainer, and immediately agreed (I had actually attended the same class a few years earlier). The individual then started to tell me all of the other reasons she had to attend the class (she had obviously put a fair amount of thought into this, and had actually prepared a list for our discussion). I cut her off almost immediately explaining that I really appreciated the fact that she had obviously put a fair amount of thought into their request, but I had already agreed; at this point the only thing she might do is talk me OUT of it.

Chapter 5: Rules

Rule 8: Understanding is the responsibility of the communicator

Think about it. If someone does not fully understand you, *but thinks that they do*, they will likely not ask for more clarification. You, as the communicator, are the only person with a full understanding of what you are communicating until you have fully satisfied yourself that the other party really understands what you are communicating to them. It is *your* fault if someone executes a task for you or proceeds in any way, incorrectly, based on what they think you told them.

Rule 9: Perception is at least as important as reality

If you do a great job on something, but your Senior or the client thinks that you did NOT do a good job, you did not do a good job. It is always your responsibility to not only produce quality work, but to also effectively communicate that quality - ALWAYS. Keep in mind that your job (as explained in Chapter 1) is to gain and retain the confidence of your boss, and the job of the firm is to gain and retain the confidence of their clients. You cannot expect to just do excellent work and blindly trust in others to recognize that excellence.

> You will likely hear, at some point, that you should strive to be "trusted business advisors" for your clients. The word "trusted" is crucial. It does your client (and you!) relatively little good if you provide the best advice in the world but you are not perceived as trustworthy.
>
> In every situation, you should obviously strive to act with the utmost integrity and professionalism; don't forget to think about how your actions are perceived.

Chapter 5: Rules

Rule 10:   Do not make a mistake by yourself

No matter the situation, you are always working as part of a team (even if you are the only person working on a particular project, you will have someone to whom you are reporting). Nobody, at any level, should make unilateral decisions. There is always at least one other individual you should be consulting when faced with an important decision. If a mistake is made, you need to make sure it is based on a decision made only after consulting with others (and by others, I mean those people above you).

Rule 11:   Persistence always works

Never quit. If the job was easy, anyone could do it.

This book did not start out as a book. It started out as a whole lot of notes I took down over the course of my career. When I came across an idea or a situation I thought was worth remembering, I (usually) wrote it down. The book you just finished does not cover everything, nor is it intended to. When you come across something you want to remember, particularly something you can pass along to others, write it down here (I have started you off with a couple that one of my long-time colleagues related to me). Again good luck, and remember – this job can be very rewarding, both personally and professionally. The more you think about what you are learning every day, the more you will appreciate that learning, and the better prepared you will be to train the next generation of professionals.

- Always keep a pen with you. It is usually easy to borrow something to write on, but not always easy to borrow something to write with.

- Keep a stain-removing pen or stain-removing wipes in your computer bag.

_____
_____
_____
_____
_____
_____
_____
_____
_____
_____
_____
_____
_____
_____
_____
_____
_____
_____
_____
_____
_____
_____
_____
_____
_____
_____
_____
_____
_____
_____

Your turn

CPSIA information can be obtained
at www.ICGtesting.com
Printed in the USA
LVOW02s1703110516
487197LV00006B/19/P